A Wonderful Sight!

The Story of Jesus and a Man Who Couldn't See

We are grateful to the following team of authors for their contributions to *God Loves Me*, a Bible story program for young children. This Bible story, one of a series of fifty-two, was written by Patricia L. Nederveld, managing editor for CRC Publications. Suggestions for using this book were developed by Jesslyn DeBoer, a freelance author from Grand Rapids, Michigan. Yvonne Van Ee, an early childhood educator, served as project consultant and wrote *God Loves Me*, the program guide that accompanies this series of Bible storybooks.

Nederveld has served as a consultant to Title I early childhood programs in Colorado. She has extensive experience as a writer, teacher, and consultant for federally funded preschool, kindergarten, and early childhood programs in Colorado, Texas, Michigan, Florida, Missouri, and Washington, using the *High/Scope* Education Research Foundation curriculum. In addition to writing the *Bible Footprints* church curriculum for four- and five-year-olds, Nederveld edited the revised *Threes* curriculum and the first edition of preschool through second grade materials for the *LiFE* curriculum, all published by CRC Publications.

DeBoer has served as a church preschool leader and as coauthor of the preschool-kindergarten materials for the *LiFE* curriculum published by CRC Publications. She has also written K-6 science and health curriculum for Christian Schools International and gift books for the Zondervan Corporation, Grand Rapids, Michigan.

Van Ee is a professor and early childhood program advisor in the Education Department at Calvin College, Grand Rapids, Michigan. She has served as curriculum author and consultant for Christian Schools International and wrote the original *Story Hour* organization manual and curriculum materials for fours and fives.

Photos on page 5 and 20: SuperStock.

Library of Congress Cataloging-in-Publication Data

Nederveld, Patricia L., 1944-
    A wonderful sight!: the story of Jesus and a man who couldn't see/
Patricia L. Nederveld.
        p. cm. — (God loves me; bk. 37)
    Summary: A retelling of the Biblical story in which Jesus
heals a man who cannot see. Includes follow-up activities.
    ISBN 1-56212-306-8
    1. Opening of the eyes of one blind at Bethsaida (Miracle)—
Juvenile literature. [1. Opening of the eyes of one blind at Bethsaida
(Miracle) 2. Jesus Christ—Miracles. 3. Bible stories—N.T.] I. Title. II. Series:
Nederveld, Patricia L., 1944- God loves me; bk. 37.
BT367.064N43   1998
232.9'55—dc21   98-16963
                                                  CIP
                                                  AC

10 9 8 7 6 5 4 3 2 1

A Wonderful Sight!

The Story of Jesus and a Man Who Couldn't See

PATRICIA L. NEDERVELD

ILLUSTRATIONS BY PATRICK KELLEY

CRC Publications
Grand Rapids, Michigan

This is a story from God's book, the Bible.

It's for <small>say name(s) of your child(ren).</small>
It's for me too!

Mark 8:22-26

Birds! Flowers! People! Trees! Colors all around us! What a wonderful sight!

Once there lived a man who couldn't see a single color or shape around him. He couldn't see birds or flowers. He couldn't see people or trees either.

Some people brought the man to Jesus. They knew Jesus could do amazing things. Maybe Jesus could make the man's eyes see again. . . .

Jesus took the man's hand and walked with him. The man wondered what Jesus looked like. And where was Jesus taking him?

J esus stopped. He put his hands on the man's eyes and said, "Do you see anything?"

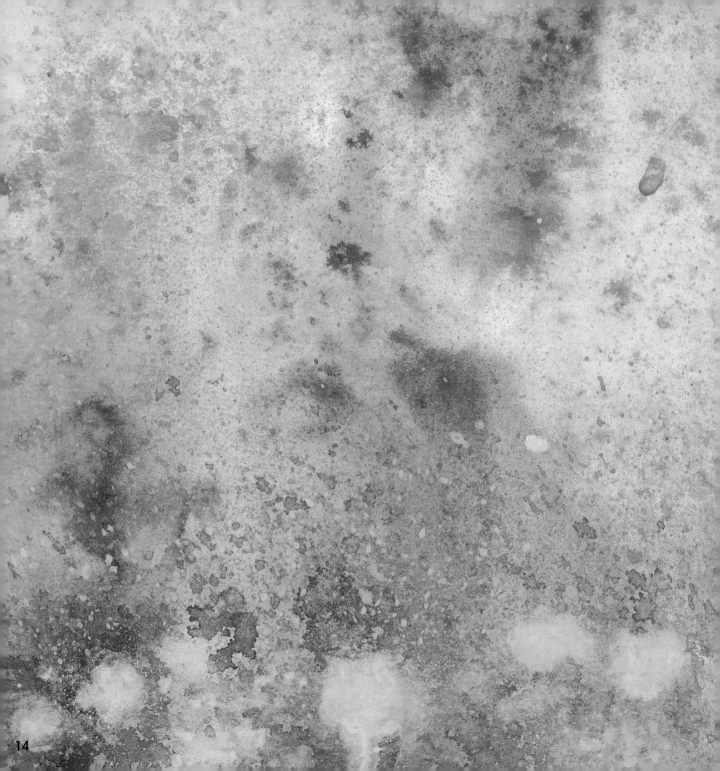

Colors!
Shapes!
Yes, he could see something . . . but not everything! "I think I see people, but they look like trees walking around," said the man.

Then Jesus touched the man's eyes again.

Birds! Flowers! People! Trees! Colors all around him. What a wonderful sight! Now he could see everything.

" Go home now," Jesus said. And the man thought about his home, his family, his friends. He wanted to *see* them, really *see* them! What a wonderful sight!

wonder what
your favorite
color is . . .

*Dear God, thank
you for giving us
wonderful colors
and shapes. Your
world is a wonderful
sight! Amen.*

Suggestions for Follow-up

Opening

As you welcome your little ones, tell them you're so happy you have eyes to see their beautiful smiles (or new shirts, or happy faces). Look for opportunities to help the children appreciate their eyes and praise God for everything they can see. Be especially sensitive to the child who may be visually impaired.

Gather your group in a circle, and ask the children to point to the part of their body they use to see. Ask the children to close their eyes and put their hands over them. Then ask them if they can point to familiar objects in the room (tables, chairs, windows, a favorite toy, and so on). Invite them to open their eyes again to check if they were right. Wonder with them what it would be like not to be able to see. Thank God for each pair of eyes.

Learning Through Play

Learning through play is the best way! The following activity suggestions are meant to help you provide props and experiences that will invite the children to play their way into the Scripture story and its simple truth. Try to provide plenty of time for the children to choose their own activities and to play individually. Use group activities sparingly—little ones learn most comfortably with a minimum of structure.

1. Let your little ones experiment with colored Play-Doh. (We've included a recipe in the suggestions for arranging and equipping the space, *God Loves Me* program guide. You will want to color half of the dough blue and the other half yellow.) Give each child a small clump of each color, and invite them to mix the two colors together. When the two are thoroughly mixed, the dough will turn green. Name the beautiful colors God made, and marvel at the wonderful eyes God gave each child to see blue and yellow and green.

2. Children who are squeamish about getting messy may enjoy making rainbow bags. Cover the table with newspaper or a shower curtain, and provide paint shirts in case of accidental leaks. Place small quantities of two or three colors of tempera paint or finger paint into small sealable plastic bags (the kind with zippers work best). Squeeze out excess air, and seal tightly. Name the colors as you show your little ones how to draw with their fingers or lightly knead the bags to mix the colors. Express delight at each child's beautiful mix of colors. Praise God that each child can see the the sun, the moon, stars, and a rainbow in God's great big sky.

3. Your little ones are beginning to recognize colors and shapes of objects in their world. In your art area, set out sheets of construction paper, glue sticks, and shapes you've cut from a variety of colored paper. Or you may prefer to purchase an assortment of colorful sticker shapes from your local craft or school supply store. Children with visual impairments can feel the shapes if you back them with sandpaper. Show the children how to make a collage of the shapes. Talk about the blue circle

or the red square as children create a design. Model wonder and thankfulness for the variety of colors and shapes we see in God's world.

4. Play a game of "I Spy." Begin by saying to one child, "I spy with my two eyes someone who is wearing a red shirt" (or playing with blocks, and so on). Ask the child to point to the right person. Then ask that child to join the two of you as you continue the game. Play enough rounds to give every child a chance to be the spy. Add a verbal clue for the child who cannot see—ask her to find the child who is pounding, singing. . . . Thank the children for helping you search so carefully.

5. One or all of your little ones can join in a game of "See and Touch." Stand in the center of the room, and instruct the players to quickly touch something that you name. It may be a toy, a book, a chair. Add colors and shapes to the description if your little ones can identify more specific objects, and add verbal clues (squeaky chair, talking book) to help the child who cannot see. Thank God for eyes and ears and hands.

6. Children may enjoy a sight/memory game too. Choose two small toys from your play area. (Older children will be able to remember more than two items.) Display the toys on a tray or table. Invite the children to look closely at the toys. Let the child who is visually impaired feel the toys. Talk about the colors and shapes. Then ask your little ones to close their eyes while you take away one of the toys. When they look again, can they tell you what toy is missing? Praise the children for using their eyes so well, and praise God with them for their ability to see.

Closing

Take a few moments to let each child respond to the question on page 21. If your children do not know colors well, display a few objects with different colors—a red ball, a green block—and let them choose the color and shape they like best. Conclude your time together with the prayer on page 21.

At Home

Young children often seem to notice the wonderful sights in God's world that adults tend to overlook. Let your little one help you rediscover the marvelous colors and shapes all around you. Take a stroll together around your neighborhood, and notice the brown circles in the middle of a flower, the grey squares or rectangles in the sidewalk, the blue oval-shaped robin's eggs, the yellow round sun or crescent moon, and so forth. Give thanks for eyes to see all the beautiful things in God's world.

Old Testament Stories

Blue and Green and Purple Too! *The Story of God's Colorful World*

It's a Noisy Place! *The Story of the First Creatures*

Adam and Eve *The Story of the First Man and Woman*

Take Good Care of My World! *The Story of Adam and Eve in the Garden*

A Very Sad Day *The Story of Adam and Eve's Disobedience*

A Rainy, Rainy Day *The Story of Noah*

Count the Stars! *The Story of God's Promise to Abraham and Sarah*

A Girl Named Rebekah *The Story of God's Answer to Abraham*

Two Coats for Joseph *The Story of Young Joseph*

Plenty to Eat *The Story of Joseph and His Brothers*

Safe in a Basket *The Story of Baby Moses*

I'll Do It! *The Story of Moses and the Burning Bush*

Safe at Last! *The Story of Moses and the Red Sea*

What Is It? *The Story of Manna in the Desert*

A Tall Wall *The Story of Jericho*

A Baby for Hannah *The Story of an Answered Prayer*

Samuel! Samuel! *The Story of God's Call to Samuel*

Lions and Bears! *The Story of David the Shepherd Boy*

David and the Giant *The Story of David and Goliath*

A Little Jar of Oil *The Story of Elisha and the Widow*

One, Two, Three, Four, Five, Six, Seven! *The Story of Elisha and Naaman*

A Big Fish Story *The Story of Jonah*

Lions, Lions! *The Story of Daniel*

New Testament Stories

Jesus Is Born! *The Story of Christmas*

Good News! *The Story of the Shepherds*

An Amazing Star! *The Story of the Wise Men*

Waiting, Waiting, Waiting! *The Story of Simeon and Anna*

Who Is This Child? *The Story of Jesus in the Temple*

Follow Me! *The Story of Jesus and His Twelve Helpers*

The Greatest Gift *The Story of Jesus and the Woman at the Well*

A Father's Wish *The Story of Jesus and a Little Boy*

Just Believe! *The Story of Jesus and a Little Girl*

Get Up and Walk! *The Story of Jesus and a Man Who Couldn't Walk*

A Little Lunch *The Story of Jesus and a Hungry Crowd*

A Scary Storm *The Story of Jesus and a Stormy Sea*

Thank You, Jesus! *The Story of Jesus and One Thankful Man*

A Wonderful Sight! *The Story of Jesus and a Man Who Couldn't See*

A Better Thing to Do *The Story of Jesus and Mary and Martha*

A Lost Lamb *The Story of the Good Shepherd*

Come to Me! *The Story of Jesus and the Children*

Have a Great Day! *The Story of Jesus and Zacchaeus*

I Love You, Jesus! *The Story of Mary's Gift to Jesus*

Hosanna! *The Story of Palm Sunday*

The Best Day Ever! *The Story of Easter*

Goodbye—for Now *The Story of Jesus' Return to Heaven*

A Prayer for Peter *The Story of Peter in Prison*

Sad Day, Happy Day! *The Story of Peter and Dorcas*

A New Friend *The Story of Paul's Conversion*

Over the Wall *The Story of Paul's Escape in a Basket*

A Song in the Night *The Story of Paul and Silas in Prison*

A Ride in the Night *The Story of Paul's Escape on Horseback*

The Shipwreck *The Story of Paul's Rescue at Sea*

Holiday Stories

Selected stories from the New Testament to help you celebrate the Christian year

Jesus Is Born! *The Story of Christmas*

Good News! *The Story of the Shepherds*

An Amazing Star! *The Story of the Wise Men*

Hosanna! *The Story of Palm Sunday*

The Best Day Ever! *The Story of Easter*

Goodbye—for Now *The Story of Jesus' Return to Heaven*

These fifty-two books are the heart of *God Loves Me*, a Bible story program designed for young children. Individual books (or the entire set) and the accompanying program guide *God Loves Me* are available from CRC Publications (1-800-333-8300).